Do You Know Who You Are?

Tiffany Harris

authorHOUSE®

AuthorHouse™
1663 Liberty Drive
Bloomington, IN 47403
www.authorhouse.com
Phone: 1 (800) 839-8640

Published by AuthorHouse 09/19/2017

ISBN: 978-1-5462-0877-8 (sc)
ISBN: 978-1-5462-0876-1 (e)

Library of Congress Control Number: 2017914252

Print information available on the last page.

Contents

Abstract

The ancestral history of my family has been studied. Using new technologies, and the DNA ancestry kit, via 23 And Me, I submitted a saliva sample for testing. I am Asa Abdullah, the sole subject of this test. I am also a twenty-eight year old wife, and mother. From this test, I have been found to be the descendant of peoples from all over. I am African, European, and Southeast Asian. I am indigenous to the Americas, Oceanian, and Iberian. Concluding this study, I have decided to write a book, introducing my lineage. With this information, I can answer lifelong questions about my past.

Dedication

To El'Shaddai my God above me. You are the creator of all things,

heaven, and earth. Let everything I do give glory to your name.

My Dad. Thanks for those bedtime stories. You've created a dreamer and an author.

My mom and brothers: Guys, here is to answer the questions

we've been asking for many years. Let's do this.

My husband Thank you for supporting me and my dreams. Love you, honey.

And to our kids: Grandma once told me "You'll never know where you're going until you

know where you've been." Here is to your bright, and prosperous, futures. Learn where

your ancestors have been and never let anyone take this from you. I love you all.

Acknowledgements

El'Shaddai, thank you, heavenly Father, for your grace, mercy, protection, and patience. I believe you've given me the gifts I have for a purpose. Your will be done.

There aren't enough words, in the English language, to express how happy I feel about this book publishing. It has taken me years to get to this point. I've written on topic, after topic; and tossed one book after another away. I wasn't satisfied with the work I had completed and wasn't going to stop until I was. I've spent countless hours negotiation prices with one publishing company, after another, to ultimately find myself unhappy with deals, and packages, in front of me. Now that I am here, I look forward to what is coming next.

Writing has always come easily to me. English was not only my favorite subject, in school, but the easiest "A" I've ever earned. I've always had a desire to find, and fight for something, and I think this book puts me on the path to where I need to be. In the chapters you will read, you will learn what this journey was like for me. You will come to understand why it is so important, and how I've come to see myself differently. I've searched for the answers to questions, about my roots. Now that I've found them, I can close this chapter in my life, and begin again; with a new one. There's no doubt I will always find something to search for. It is in my nature. I seek the unknown. This journey wouldn't be complete without the help of a ton of wonderful people behind me. I've been raised to "give credit where credit is due," so to the following people; thank you. To Tim Murphy of Author House Publishers, you deserve a big "thank you." Had it not been for the work you've done, this book might never have. Your level of commitment is truly inspiring. There's nothing like a person who gets the job done, and you fella, are that guy. To my team who helped me get through this project. Thanks for your dedication and devotion. No one rises without the help of someone willing to aid them on their way up. To my check in coordinator, thanks for keeping me on my toes. There were days when I felt like dragging this process out a little longer. Our talk on March 29, 2017, motivated me to get to work

Prologue

History is by far one of the most important aspects of any society. From it, we learn all of mankind's accomplishments and failures. We learn of war, peace, conquerings, traditions, and customs. Laws are written and change the course of history. Movements shake the foundations of civilizations and rewrite what once was history, to be history in the making. Mankind reflects on history to learn from it. He, and often she, pushes boundaries, takes risks, and overcomes oppression; all of which is written on the pages of history books. Man has studied the stars, sailed the seas, and set foot on land he never knew before. Until now, mankind has studied the history of a collective whole, with few exceptions, but he hasn't studied the history of me.

Scientific advances forever changed our view of history. The once unknown now can be explained. Scientists have discovered a number of things; among many, the human DNA. Our genetics have been tested and rooted more broadly than we once imagined. Today, anyone questioning their lineage doesn't have to move half way around the world, to find answers. Science has given us a way to use our DNA to look into the past, and read the pages of history again. However, when reading a second time, the history becomes more personal. We are able to travel the globe, one chromosome at a time, and discover something meaningful. We can discover the history of me, us, the individual in the mirror. We learn of the accomplishments and failures of those before us and unlock the limitless potential within. I began the journey to self-discovery, some time ago. In the glory of a rough, and hopeless childhood, I knew if I could find within myself, the power to achieve, I could do anything I wanted. I believe that energy has been passed down to me. It came from the slaves who sought freedom. From the ancient world where architecture was built, but that we, to this day, are scratching our heads trying to figure out how they did it. It flows through my veins, beats in my heart every time someone tries to get me to doubt myself, as a reminder of what lies within me. It is in me, as it was in them; those who came before me and did the unthinkable. Today, I begin again. I begin a new journey. This time, I set out to recapture the history I never knew. I set out to see myself in the eyes of the people of the world. I yearn to walk the lands my ancestors traveled. While the world around is focused on the history of others, today I begin to write the history of me.

Chapter 1

Birth of the Racially Ambiguous

I made my first appearance November 27, 1988. Born the youngest of five children in a Colorado hospital, our family was complete. After years of birthing the boys she so loved, my mother finally had a girl. We were outnumbered, with my father and four boys, but we were a family nonetheless. The funny thing is what happened when my mother first saw me. After some extended time cleaning, and even losing me in the hospital, the nurses laid me in my mother's arms. Though to her surprise, I was as pale as ever, with blonde hair and blue eyes. Something wasn't right. An African American woman and her Middle Eastern-looking husband birthed a white baby. Was this their kid? Had it not been for the hospital bracelet on my ankle and the matching one on her wrist, this place would have had a lawsuit on its hands! My mom thought she was given the wrong baby. I think we're all familiar with those cases of kids being "accidentally" switched at birth. So where did my pale skin, blonde hair, and blue eyes come from?

The thing about DNA is that it is sort of complicated. Many beliefs exist about DNA, and about how a child inherits what from their parents. Science proves DNA and genetic inheritance to be more difficult to understand than we know. For example, if two parents, with two different blood types, have children, then the child may not inherit a blood type identical to either parent. If mom is O, dad is AB, the children may come out with either parent's blood type-or simply A or B. The greatest example of this is my own son. His father is AB, and I am O; our son is A. However, the confusion doesn't end there. Each of our parents gives us two genes. We get one from mom, and one from dad, who each inherited one gene from their mothers and one from their fathers. From this each pass one to their children. Quoted it can be explained this way, "Simply we get these genes from our parents, it is common to share traits with our parents, like blood type. But like I said at the start, that's not always the case. Because we have two copies of the blood type gene and there are three possible versions of this gene, there are six possible combinations. Officially complicated!" Danielle Dondanville, *Eye Color, Hair Color, Bloody Types, and Other Traits,* The Tech Museum of Innovation. Web. 6 December 2016. All humans have the same

20,000 or more genes. We're uniquely separated by many versions of these genes. We all have the blood type ABO, and from this blood types A, B, and O. I know what you're thinking, *oh, so simply put, all humans have one of the three blood types.* No, that's not how it works, as Danielle Dondanville explained. The various versions of blood types can be anything from AA to AO, or AB to O, or anything in between. Sort of complicated, right? Our eye color, skin tone, hair color, and texture are all determined by DNA.

DNA determined that my eyes would be blue, although both of my parents have brown eyes. How is this? Summarized, a number of colors can "lurk" behind the eyes of brown eyed parents. Green, blue, hazel, gray, etc., all can exist in the gene pool of the two. However, in order for a blue eyed child, to come from brown eyed parents, the gene must show up at the "right" time, to produce blue, from brown. If only one parent has the "blue eye" gene, no child will directly inherit baby blues. Still, the children carry the gene to produce blue eyes, in their children. Stanford University's Dr. Barry Star explains further, "This is one way that blue eyes can stay hidden for hundreds of years before making a sudden, dramatic appearance. Only one parent in each generation has blue hidden behind his or her brown. Now, generation after generation, everyone will have brown eyes, and some will have those hidden blues. The blue eyes would keep getting passed down until finally one of the "carriers of blue eyes" had children with another parent that was a carrier, too. Now their children would have a chance at blue eyes." Dr. Barry Star, *"Eye Color, Hair Color, Blood Types, and Other Traits"* The Tech Museum of Innovations. Web. 3, Dec. 2014. Meaning, my parents, though both brown eyed, are "carriers" for the "blue eyes" gene. The gene showed up at the "right" time, when I was conceived, and thus the answer to my question. The gene was passed, I know, from my paternal grandmother to my father, and on to me. Still, an even more interesting discovery takes us deeper on our quest for the "blue eyes" gene. Que the OCA2! Formerly known as the "P" gene, the OCA2 is the gene that provides instructions for making the P protein. The OCA2 also is responsible for the production of melanin and gives us our hair, skin, and eye color. U.S. National Library of Medicine *OCA2 Melanosomal Transmembrane Protein,* Web. 19, July 2017. We further discuss the "P" gene in chapter 4.

While this information is amazing, it isn't what the book is about. We've come to understand (to a point) how genes work regarding personal features, but what about our ethnicity? What part does DNA play in our ethnic makeup? How have we come to see ourselves as a color on a social construct, but lost sight of who we are ethnically? All our lives we've been asked to identify ourselves under the banner of "race," but what is race? Is it biological, or a manmade idea? We'll answer this question in chapter 2, as we examine this thing called "race," and why I feel the need to break away from it.

CHAPTER 2

Race: Biological or Not? What Science Says

What is race? Scientists have argued this for quite some time. Is it a social construct, wherein groups of people are classified as having similar heritage (e.g. African Americans having ancestry throughout the continent of Africa)? Or is it a way of classifying people based on biological factors, such as how one may or may not react to some form of medical treatment or a drug. Does it have insight into one group of people's risk factors for contracting certain biological diseases? Dr. Ann Mornings addressed this in her article, "Does Genomes Challenge the Social Construct of Race?" Morning debates the findings of Shiao and his colleagues, regarding the beliefs of "constructionists." Such is described as not being "up to date", with an emphasis on an amendment. While Dr. Mornings does recognize the role of biology in "race", she also argues this is limited, but also gives way to discrimination of some, by others. "In contrast, I submit that the constructionist theory is not blind to the input that human biology can have in racial classification, but that it rejects as empirically unwarranted the genetic determination, or racial categories Shiao et. al.'s (2012) assertion of a "biological basis" (p.68) for race at time implies." Mornings, Ann "Does Genomes Challenge the Social Construction of Race," Sociological Theory 2014. *DAI* 32:189. Print. Such constructionist beliefs are summed up as follows: "Constructionist theories of race thus portray biological differences between different groups as a byproduct of social classification practices, not as their driver or even major contributor. In the constructionist perspective, categories are fashioned and meaning according to sociopolitical imperatives-for example, who is native to a territory and who is a settler; who can be enslaved and who cannot; who is a member of the faithful, ruling clan, or superior stock." Mornings, Ann "Does Genomes Challenge the Social Construction of Race," Sociological Theory 2014. *DAI* 32: 189. Print. From this we can understand the following to be true, those who fall into racial categories viewed as "superior" have free reign to particular regions, and all in their reach. On the flip side, those further down, and even living at the bottom of the hierarchy are beholden to the power of those "superior" to them. This gives way to racial supremacy groups such as the American Neo-Nazi Party, and the ICGC (Israel Church of God in Christ). Some of what I've learned while writing this book does point to a biological aspect of the human DNA and can be found in some races, more than others. The OCA2 and blue eyes, as studied by Dr. Hans Eiberg, for example. Still, Dr. Mornings further illustrates why the constructionists argue biology is limited in racial categorizing. "Racial constructionism offers several explanations for why a deterministic mapping of biology to race is indefensible. First, neither historical origins nor the malleability of racial categories supports the claim that they 'have a biological basis in statistically discernable clusters of alleles' (Shiao et. al. 2012: 68). The 'white' category, for example, has expanded and contracted so dramatically over time- to include or exclude Jews, Irish people, Laplanders, Hispanics, South Asians, Middle Easterners, and Ethiopians for example (Hanley-Lopez 1996; Jacobson 1998; Marks 1995; Samhan 1999; Sanders 1969) –that it is hard to discern the 'biological reality' at work." Mornings, Ann "Does Genomes Challenge the Social Construction of Race", Sociology Theory 2014. *DAI* 32:189 Print.

The "constructionist" view on "race" gives rise to an unfair classification system. This rings true to the treatment of some groups, by others, throughout American history. At one time, only "white" Anglo-Saxon males who owned land, could vote. That is, only those with the means, and who belonged to the "right race" and gender, were allotted these privileges. However, women were seen as inferior, less intelligent, and incapable of being part of the voting system. African Americans, male and female, were once viewed as sub-human, and they had been classified at the same level as animals. Still, the question remains whether or not there are biological factors that explain the notion of "race" and if so, why we abide by it? Mornings argues against this belief when she states: "Underscoring this point, the focus of this article will be on examining Shiao et al.'s (2012) main argument that current research in human genetics warrants a reformulation of constructivist race theory. As it turns out, review of the scientific literature they cite reveals how deeply social the production of this strand of biological knowledge is. There are myriad ways in which 'facts' about human genetic variation are shaped by analysts' assumptions and decisions: Choices about whose DNA to sample and which types of genetic data to analyze, as well as assumptions about how different populations are related to each other and decisions about what statistical techniques to employ, all bear on scientists' conclusions about the genetic "clusters" that ostensibly characterize our species. Moreover, they leave many openings for our widely shared beliefs about racial difference to filter in. Consequently, the examination of research reports in human genetics leads me to contest Shiao et al.'s claim that recent research has clearly demonstrated "that certain racial, and also ethnic, categories have a biological basis in statistically discernible clusters of alleles" (Shiao et al. 2012:68). Instead, statistically inferred human genetic clusters have a social basis that is entirely consistent with current constructivist thinking about race. Our depictions of the genetic structure of human populations are themselves so culturally conditioned that it would be a mistake to conclude that they represent objective biological measurements that are any less a human artifact than folk taxonomies." Morning, Ann "Does Genomes Challenge the Social Construction of Race," Sociology Theory 2014. *DAI* 32:189.In her own words, Morning argues that Shiao and colleagues' claims are unfounded and biased; she claims that the findings are based on particular practices, proceedings, and modes of exercise. So, does science prove there is no biology in "race"?

A counter argument has been offered by Nicholas Wade in his article, "What Science Says About Race and Genetics," published in Time Magazine. While Mornings argues there are flaws in the method by which we classify specific races, Wade offers an explanation. He states, "Analysis of genomes from around the world establishes that there is a biological basis for race, despite the official statements to the contrary of leading social science organizations. An illustration of the point is the fact that with mixed race populations, such as African Americans, geneticists can now track along an individual's genome, and assign each segment to an African or European ancestor, an exercise that would be impossible if race did not have some biological reality." Wade, Nicholas "What Science Says About Race and Genetics," Time.com. 09, May 2014. Web.

Jacqueline Howard, senior science editor for the Huffington Post, wrote on this issue, in her article "What Scientists Mean When They Say Race Is Not Genetic." According to her research, scientist feel, "the problem of race in such research is 'problematic at best and harmful at worst.'" Howard, Jacqueline What Scientists Mean When They Say Race Is Not Genetic. Huffington Post, 09, Feb. 2016. Web. What does this mean? For more than a century, race has been used as a method to biologically classify groups of people. However, scientists like Francis Collins, the head of the National Genome Research Institute, calls these practices "flawed." She goes so far as to call race a "weak" concept, and suggest science move beyond it. W.E.B. Dubois joined the debate 100 years ago, arguing against the concept of classifying people as "black," or "white." Still, classification of people, by "race" continues. If Nicholas Wade is correct, in his assessment, then anthropologist in the Kennewick Man's case should've been able to label the skull, by race, and show the remains to belong to someone white, black, etc. The 1996 discovery of an ancient skeleton, in the Pacific Northwest, sparked controversy, as scientists set out to discover the "race" of the remains. Native residents of the area sued anthropologist for the head of an unidentified human, one the tribe claimed belonged to their people. The courts agreed, in accordance with the Department of Interior under federal law that provides Natives the right to claim all pre-European remains, if cultural affiliation can be established. Determined anthropologists filed suit, asking to be allowed to study the head. Why? According to forensic anthropologist George

5

W. Gill, this type of study can often be used to determine the race of skeleton. "We produce as much accuracy in race as we do in sex and age." Lawson, William "Anthropologists Disagree About Race and Bones" ABCNews.com. Cable News Network, 06 Oct. 2000.Web. Gill is one of only 60 certified forensic anthropologists in the United States and Canada that assist in crime detection, using evidence found on dead bodies. George Gill seems very proud of his work, and sure of his capabilities, but others disagree with his claims. Michigan State University professor Norman Saucer couldn't be sold on the concept of race. Saucer explained "race" to be a human invention, with which we've endured as a societal concept, but one that cannot be defined. He goes further to state, "If you were to walk from Europe to Africa, where do you put the line? All change is gradual. The lines are historical and political. It's in people's minds." Lawson, William "Anthropologist Disagree About Race and Bones," ABCNews.com. Cable News Network, 06 Oct. 2000. Web. If "race" is a human invention, a classification system, we may better understand the claims of "trans-racialism" made by infamous Rachel Dolezal.

Former NAACP Civil Rights activist and Africana Studies instructor Rachel Dolezal, became a household name when outed by parents, Ruthanne and Lawrence Dolezal. Their "white" born daughter had been living a lie. Rachel fooled everyone she'd come in contact with into believing she was "black." Dolezal explained she identified as "black" and argued "race" is a social construct, not a biological feature. When asked if she was African American, Rachel responded, "No." However, in 2017 she adopted an African name. What did Ms. Dolezal mean when she called "race" a construct?

Michael Omi and Howard Winant explore "race" and how it shaped American society in their book, "Racial Formation in the United States: From the 1960s to the 1990s." Omi et. al. introduce the three approaches to "race"; nationality, ethnicity, and class. From each of these came new ideals, and even questions against Social Darwinism. One argument stated that ethnic minorities could be introduced into society, the same way white had been. Of course, no belief is developed without a counter. On the subject of ethnicity I quote, "The ethnicity-based paradigm arose in the 1920s and 1930s as an explicit challenge to the prevailing racial views of the period. The pre-existing biologistic paradigm had evolved since the downfall of racial slavery to explain racial inferiority as a part of a natural order of humankind. Whites were considered a superior race; white skin was the norm while other skin colors were exotic mutations which had to be explained. Race was equated with distinct hereditary characteristics. Differences in intelligence, temperament, and sexuality (among other traits) were deemed to be racial in character. Racial intermixing was seen as a sin against nature which would lead to the creation of 'biological throwbacks.' These were some of the assumptions in social Darwinists, Spencerists, and eugenicists thinking about race and race relations." (p.14) Omi, Michael, Howard Winant, "Race Formation in the United States: From the 1960s to the 1990s," 2nd Ed. New York; Routledge, 1994. Print. Ideas like this give way to racism and discrimination. We've seen it with the introduction of segregation, the Jim Crow laws, and miscegenation laws that forbade intermixed marriage.

Regardless what you believe, whether you think race is man-made or biological, we cannot hide the ugly history and inhumane treatment of one another, justified by "race." We've made much progress over time. However, we still have a way to go. Recent events prove we're not too evolved from the racist thoughts of those before us. I, for one, believe "race" is not biological. I feel this way because of the outstanding evidence that proves otherwise. While we're on the subject of "race," we may as well tackle the ugly elephant in the room, racism. One thing I've learned about prejudice is this, it comes from all sides. Whites are prejudice to black and brown people, but black and brown people are also bigoted against whites. Blacks discriminate against other blacks, based on skin tone, and Willie Lynch syndrome thinking. It's something I've seen, felt, and experience. It's also something we need to get rid of.

Chapter 3

Race and Racism, Prejudice from All Sides.

The following chapter touches on race. We're all too familiar with it (race) and the problems regarding race relations. These issues affect us, how we see and treat each other, and how society functions as a whole. Each of us has a tale of our own personal experiences about race. However, I want to introduce an aspect bigotry we ignore; intraracial prejudice. It isn't often we hear of discrimination within a particular race by own. The following stories touch on prejudice on both fronts. Racism is not a one sided issue, prejudice hits from all sides. Note that while some of these stories deal with intraracial prejudice, others forms of bigotry are discussed.

Sydney is a misunderstood child. A fair skinned, kinky haired beauty; she's an outcast among her peers. Sydney struggles to fit in. She's not "black" enough for those in her neighborhood. She never has been. Colorism runs deep in her community, but Sydney falls on the side we never discuss; the prejudicial treatment of light skinned blacks. While she would grow listening to the cries of "unfair" and "unjust" treatment, from her darker counterparts, she too would be a victim. Sydney was introduced to "race" in third grade. At the time she attended a predominately black school in New York. Few whites attended Parkway Elementary. In fact, there was only one white child in her class. His name was Simon. One day, Sydney and Simon were paired together for an assignment. Rather than talk about their work, Simon babbled on nonstop. During the course of their one sided conversation, as he rambled on and she pretended to listen, Simon said something Sydney couldn't ignore. "You know they'll never really like us? You and me, they hate us because we're white." Sydney is African American, but can pass for just about anything. Her racially ambiguous features are misleading. "Wait, I'm not white," Sydney replied. Though shocking, it came as no surprise Simon felt this way. In a neighborhood of chocolate skin Sydney stood out. Acceptance was hard to find for a light skinned girl.

Racial tensions gave way to more negative human interaction. In a more civilized surrounding, conflict resolution skills are taught. Children and adults alike learn to solve their problems through dialogue. Unfortunately, this wasn't the case. Sydney's environment was riddled with violence and crime, and as any psychologist will tell you; human behavior is shaped by environment. Violence was the solution to any and all problems. In fourth grade she was the target of a group who wanted to jump her. Sydney's family moved to a housing projects New York City. She and her brother Tyler began attending school that fall. Being the new kid is never easy, but for Sydney it was especially difficult. Making friends didn't come natural for her. So she didn't do much socializing. While the other children would hang out after school, she'd go to school and head home. Soon she became the target. In her neighborhood lived a group of aggressive girls. Among them was an African girl named Aaida. Aaida and her friends were tormenters, but she was the ring leader. She'd bullied just about everyone in the school. When Tyler and Sydney arrived, Aaida saw us a "fresh meat." She and her friends hated them because we were light skinned. Sydney had long hair and light eyes, which often gave way to unwanted attention. Girls hated her "exotic" looks because the boys they wanted seemed to love hers. Aaida was used to pushing other kids around with no push back. However, unlike the others, Tyler and Sydney stood up to her. Things escalated and so did threats to Sydney. "She said she's not gona let some light skinned chick show her up," as she was told. Before any harm could come her way, Sydney's mother got involved and so did school authorities. Aadia and her friends backed off. The following February Sydney's father transferred his children to another school. Soon after, the family settled in nearby community.

From the first day it was obvious Sydney would be a loner. She'd met the neighborhood kids; there was Savannah, her neighbor's daughter, Tameka, Savannah's best friend, and twins Sophie and Stephanie. Sydney and Stephanie were classmates. The girls had a lot in common, yet they were very different. All were poor, black, and living in the projects. This should have given them reason to bond. It didn't. However, their differences are why Sydney was hated. She was one of two girls with a father in the home, but her parents were married. Savannah's mother was the "other woman," living with a married man. Sophie and Stephanie hadn't seen their father since he walked out a year prior, and Tameka was being raised by her sick grandmother. Sydney had long hair, while her peers wore weaves. Looks are important to girls, if you can't grow your hair to an "acceptable" length it can be upsetting. The girls accessorized with extensions and it upset them Sydney achieved the length they aspired to, naturally.

A divide existed in the minds of Tameka's crew. Somehow, being black determined everything about your life; your friends, speech patterns, and attitude. Manipulation as a weapon was used to stir the pot, or alienate an "enemy." Tameka once tried to bait Sydney to say something about Savannah's boyfriend, Andy. The two were classmates and friends, but Sydney didn't know he was *seeing* anyone. "Girl, look at him. He's cute, don't you think he's cute?" Fully aware she was being

9

baited Sydney walked away. She'd been warned how girls are, "Watch what you say around them. Girls love to gossip and these little things love to start trouble." Her mother's generalization was true, girls love to gossip. However, she noticed a difference of attitude, in her white friends and black peers. The white girls were loving of one another. They accepted their friends as they were, flaws and all. There was no backbiting in their circle. If they didn't like you, they stayed away. The black girls, on the other hand, were vicious. The closer you were to them, the easier it was to destroy you. There was never a time when they were in the same space without an altercation or argument. Stephanie was usually the cause of trouble. Sophie, Stephanie, and Tameka has a zero tolerance policy for "white washed" black girls. Judging by their mothers' example, any woman who didn't fit the negative, black stereotypes needed correction. The girls misconstrued idea of "black loyalty" showed in their disdain for any African American girls with white friends. Shardae, a fifth grade classmate was the subject of many "sell out" rants. She didn't live in the projects, her father was a surgeon, her mother an attorney. Shardae was afforded a comfortable and prosperous life. Likewise, her friends, the daughters of rich businessmen and judges, grew in luxury. All having this in common, Shardae and made friends with those of the same stock. It upset Tameka and her friends to see Shardae, a rich black girl, associating with judge's daughters; rather than joining their circle. While most school aged children played at recess, Tameka and her friends gossiped. The topic differed from day to day, but eventually, it was Shardae. "Look at that bitch," Sophie said. "She think she's white. All she do is hang with them, white girls." "Yeah," Stephanie chimed in. "She needs to come over here with her real friends," Tameka added, damn near yelling across the yard. At the time Sydney was playing with a girl named Megan. Megan was also white. Overhearing the conversation, the girls stopped. From the look on her face, Sydney could tell Megan was confused. She looked at Shardae and her friends, they seemed happy Shardae was black, her friends white, but that didn't mean they couldn't be friends. If Tameka and her gang felt this way about her, the feeling had to be the same about Sydney.

Puberty brought on the want for romantic relationships. Girls eyed boys, hoping to catch their attention, and boys tried hard to get their girl of interest. Girls became competitive over boys. Lies were told to make their "competition" seem less desirable. Each child developed a personal preference. Some boys liked skinny girls, others like "thick" ones. Some boys like tall girls, others like their women short. Some boys liked dark girls; others liked light, mixed, and/or white girls. This was somehow an issue. No one complained when the neighborhood boys wanted the chocolate girl. The other girls knew *if he's interested he'll show it*. Most were fine not being the apple of every guy's eye, the same cannot be said for their darker counterparts. Dark girls' resentment toward light skinned girls grew. Any guy who showed an interest in a light skinned or mixed girl was called, "color struck." "These niggas only want them light skinned chicks cause they can't get a white girl," It was often assumed. When a black boy dated a white girl, he was a "sell out." Somehow the notion of a mixed race relationship was explained away by a "hatred" of self, and one's mother. Mixed race discrimination hit home when Sydney's brother Trevor began dating an Irish girl. She was sweet and they made a lovely couple. However, both Sydney and her mom had to come to his defense when Trevor's choice in love was questioned by blacks. Criticism poured in from all sides, "I saw Trevor in the mall with some ugly white girl." "I just can't understand why, with all these black girls around here, he had to get one of *them.*" Perhaps the worst of it came from family, "I saw Trevor the other day with some white girl. I know you don't let your sons date them, do you?" I can think of few things worse than discrimination, in love, especially when race is involved.

Perhaps the most heartbreaking stories are of those denied love. Such is the case of middle schooler, Bethany. She hit the "my first boyfriend" milestone, started seeing a black boy, and seemed very happy. A few weeks after their relationship started, it was over. Her mom found out about Bethany's boyfriend and made them break up. The question is, why? Her anger came out in the school's gymnasium locker room. "I hate that bitch," she screamed. Curious passers stopped in their tracks. Teen drama was common at Liberty Middle School, but Bethany's outburst was out of the ordinary. A concerned friend asked, "What's going on?" News broke Bethany's mom made her break up with her boyfriend. Why? Could it be their age? Was Bethany irresponsible, or not trustworthy? Was her mother concerned she was too fragile to handle a breakup? No. The ugly truth is she didn't want her daughter dating a black guy. This happens to often. Ninth grader Mandy found her lover victimized by anti-interracial bigotry. A confrontation over race mixing took place at Fitzgerald High. Mandy, and her athlete boyfriend Reggie had been dating only a few short weeks. She was white dating a black football player and some white guys didn't like that. Tensions came to boil fall 2003 when a passerby walked upon four guys arguing. Two black, and two white, apparently sick of each other decided to have words. "You see my hair," one white guy began rubbing his bald head, "do you know what this means?" Easily explained, the guy was a skin head. After a brief exchange, both parties went their separate way. However, the conflict wasn't over. Word got around fast about the dispute. So the white guys were mad because a black guy was dating a white girl. Their "stay away from our women" buttons were triggered, and they acted on it. Thankfully, no one got hurt. Unfortunately, bigotry turned violent, with another interracial couple at the center. Fitzgerald High was full of amazing girls; but a soft spoken sandy blonde named Bella stood out. Bella was kind and polite, and loved by everyone. It came as no surprise when she caught the eye of a star athlete. He was tall, yet gentle; a studious teen, and popular. He was also African American. Bella's relationship to a black, star athlete may have been the epitome of a teen love affair, but it was an issue to some. A few guys didn't take kindly to a black guy dating a white girl. What is known is an argument broke out between Bella's ball playing beau and two white guys. One thing led to another and things started to get intense.

School administration intervened before a fight started on school grounds. Later that night, the boyfriend was due on the basketball court, but prior to the game was assaulted. After school staff broke up the would be fight, the boys plotted vengeance on the boyfriend. As he readied himself for the game, the two entered the locker room and jumped him. To make matters worse, the cowards transferred school the next day. Bella was heartbroken.

This chapter wouldn't be complete without sharing my personal experiences. I've been hit from both sides with prejudicial treatment. I've been the target of intraracial bigotry because I'm light skinned. The possibility I have a white mom or dad added fuel to the fire. I've had to walk a fine line in expression of my "blackness." After all, I was dark enough to be black, but not so dark that I could say it loud, like James Brown. All my life I'd been asked *what* my father is. His ethnicity was an issue for my African American grandmother, some of my peers, and anyone who thought he wasn't black. The thought of a non-black rearing "black" kids upset the greater population of African Americans, in my neighborhood. Before September 11, 2001, people believed he was Puerto Rican. After, people panicked thinking he was an Arab Muslim. In fact, our landlord at the time interrogated our next door neighbors, who were our friends, with one question after the next about our race, religion, and citizenship status. We were American born, all of us, but since then we've become an "exotic family of foreigners." Years later I met my husband in college. It's a day I'll never forget. I was on my way to an early class when I heard a masculine, angelic voice behind me speak. "Excuse me miss, can I talk to you?" I turned around to see him standing there in all his glory. His handsome face met mine. I studied him, from head to toe, as he spoke to me. He had a beautifully chiseled jaw, strong shoulders, and the most hypnotic brown eyes. This man was perfection. Our conversation escapes me, but we exchanged numbers and he promised to call later that day. I walked to class thinking about him, but wait, *what was his name again*? I was living at home at the time. I knew my mother would want to know about this perfect stranger. Arriving home I told her, "Mom, I met this guy today. He's really nice." "Oh, what's his name?" I didn't want to tell her I didn't know so I told her more about him. "Uh, he works on campus and has the prettiest eyes." "Ok, but what's his name?" This went on for some time before I had to tell her I didn't know. "He has my number. He said he would call me." "Ok, but Tiff, how are you going to know it's him when you don't remember his name?" We both laughed. All I knew was his name started with an M. Was it, Marcus, he didn't look like a *Marcus. Matthew*, no *Malachi*? Thankfully, in the middle of my one player name game, he called introducing himself as *Michael*. We'd started to see more of each other. I looked forward to my morning commutes to West Virginia State University where I attended college. I wanted to see him, and he lived close by. We grew close to one another, and I'd often spend my free time at his apartment. Before long his apartment became my home, and we became parents. MySpace.com was popular at the time and I had an account. Not a day went by without me uploading a picture of our little family. It was a picture of Michael, myself, and our oldest daughter Aaliyah, that sparked a race mix rant from my grandmother. "I saw a picture of Tiffany on something called 'MySpace.' She's got a boyfriend and a baby. Is he white? I can't believe you let your children deal with white people?" Anyone who knows my mother can guess how this went. "Whatever color he is I don't give a damn. That's not my business or yours, for that matter. All I care about is how he treats my daughter, how she treats him, and that they take care of my grandbaby."

In the twenty-first century, we'd all like to believe racism is a thing of the past. Well, it isn't. This chapter proves it. What I hope it also proves is that a racist can be anyone. Racism and bigotry aren't exclusive to any one race, not black, white, red, yellow, or brown. My experiences may differ with someone else's and that's fine, but I believe the lesson will be the same. You can't judge a book by its cover, nor is it ever ok to mistreat someone based on their skin color. If you take nothing else from this book, please carry this with you. I've seen racism from whites and blacks. I've been the target of anti-race mixing rants, by my own kin. A friend once told me her mother would disown her if she ever brought home a white man. I'd walked away from bigoted friends who found amusement in committing hate crimes against white women. All this madness and more showed me we still have a long way to go before race relations improve. To fix one race's bigoted attitude isn't going to wholly fix the problem of racism. Each of us has to do our part to end discrimination against our fellow man. We're different, but we all matter.

CHAPTER 4

A Closer Look at Genetic Testing

March 3, 2017, after much anticipation, I filled a small tube with my saliva. A week or so before I ordered a genetic testing kit from 23andme. Days later, I pulled my kit from the mailbox, and hurried inside. Anxiety passed as I read and followed steps one to six. One minute I was excited to take this test; the next, I was nervous what it may show. I'd spent weeks logging online live videos expressing my desire to know more about my heritage; now that I was here it felt surreal. What would I do next? How would I spend my time waiting for the results? Could I be more of one thing than another? Science Magazine Latin American correspondent Lizzie Wade, discussed genetics testing in her article on the subject. *"Researchers have found that a significant percentage of African-Americans, European Americans, and Latinos carry ancestry from outside their self-identified ethnicity."* Lizzie Wade "Genetics Study Reveals Surprising Ancestry of Many American," Sciencemag.org. 18, Dec. 2014. Wade explains, although America's three main groups self-identify as African, European, or Latino Americans, genetic testing shows that each group carries high rates of DNA outside their self-identified race. *"The average African-American genome, for example, is 73.2% African, 24% European, and 0.8% Native American.".* Lizzie Wade "Genetics Study Reveals Surprising Ancestry of Many American," Sciencemag.org. 18, Dec. 2014. Web. My Ancestry Composition Report shows similar results. The study also found genomes, and lineage percentages, vary by region. When testing southern whites, 23andme researchers found that, *"In South Carolina and Louisiana 12% of European Americans have at least 1% African ancestry. In Louisiana, too, about 8% of European Americans carry at least 1% Native American ancestry."* Lizzie Wade "Genetics Study Reveals Surprising Ancestry of Many Americans," Sciencemag.org 18, Dec. 2014. Web.

The above analysis would explain the connection between my African ancestry and blue eyes. I can't count the times I've been asked where I get my "cat eyes." Now I know, it comes from my European kin. Interestingly enough, I happened upon something amazing while conducting research for this book. Did you know all blue eyed people are related? Neither did I, but according to research we are (to some degree.) Jeanna Bryner, managing editor for LiveScience.com wrote a piece on the relation between blue eyed people, and a common European ancestor in her article, "One Common Ancestor Behind Blue Eyes." *"People with blue eyes have a single, common ancestor, according to new research. A team of scientists has tracked down a genetic mutation that leads to blue eyes."* Bryner, Jeanna. "One Common Ancestor Behind Blue Eyes," LiveScience.com 31, Jan. 2008. Web. Bryner's article focused on the research conducted by Hans Eiberg and his colleagues. In his research, Hans Eiberg of the Department of Cellular and Molecular Geneticist and Medicine at the University of Copenhagen, found between 6,000 and 10,000 years ago the *OCA2* gene mutated. Until this occurred, everyone had brown eyes. Before we go any further we need to understand the *OCA2,* and how it works. The *OCA2,* also called the "P Gene", is responsible for the production of melanin. It is from this gene we get the color of our hair, skin, and eyes. As previously stated, until a mutation in the "P Gene" caused the production of blue eyes, everyone's eyes were brown. When the mutation occurred, it didn't completely stop the production of melanin. Rather it switched the gene, causing it to produce blue in the iris, instead of brown. Further research, conducted by Hans's team showed that peoples in places such as Denmark, Turkey and Jordan have the same Haplotypes; or the same *small group of alleles of different genes (as the major histocompatibility complex) on a single chromosome that are closely enough linked to be inherited usually as a unit.* (Haplotypes, 2017) What this means is people in those regions have the same mutation, in the same spot of the DNA. Whether they know it or not, this makes them related. Apparently, my family stretches further than I once believed.

With the rise in genetic testing kits, one must wonder how DNA can be broken down to determine the specifics. Leslie O'Hanlon questioned (technologyreview.com) such testing and its accuracy. *"So I'm fascinated by the potential knowledge I could gain from this new generation of tests for genetic ancestry. But before I fork over more than $200 for such a test, the skeptic in me needs answers. What can a DNA test really tell me about where I come from? How do these tests work? And can they be wrong?" Is it possible to use one's saliva to determine ancestry? If so, how?"* O'Hanlon, Leslie "Tracing Your Ancestry," technologyreviews.com 24, Feb. 2006. Web. Four and a half weeks into the process, I'd visited my 23andme profile for an update. It was there I learned how the process works. Genetics testing involves the mitochondrial DNA, which we inherit from our mother. The mitochondrial DNA is submitted for analysis, and processed a number of ways, then put through the ringer of tests. Through the course of 6 to 8 weeks, the MTDNA is dissected to trace the individual's ancestry. Scientists test the mitochondrial DNA because unlike the *Y* chromosome, it is passed from mother to child; regardless of sex. Only boys and men carry the *Y* chromosome. For this reason, a woman can learn which genes she inherited from her father, but not his Haplotype results. Why, because females don't carry the chromosome needed for this test. If I wish to know my father's Haplotype, he needs to submit a sample. As for the mitochondrial, it goes through the following process: "*Our CLIA-certified lab experts extract DNA from the cells in your saliva sample. The lab processes the DNA on a genotyping chip that reads hundreds of thousands of variants in your genome. Your genetic data is analyzed, and we generate your personalized reports based on well-established scientific and medical research.*"23 And Me "How Your DNA Becomes A Report," 23andme.com. 2017.Web.

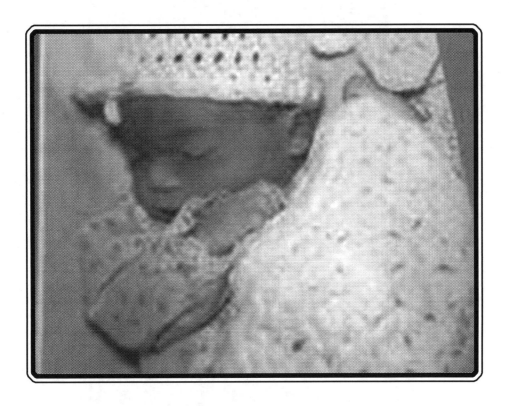

Amiyah A. Hughes, my niece. Amiyah passed away September 23, 2005. Many questions come to mind, but sadly we'll never know what caused her untimely death.

Emmanuel Jones-Isabelle, my nephew. Emmanuel Manny Jones-Isabelle was born June 29, 2010. He died March 24, 2012 at one and a half. In his short life, Manny touched the hearts of everyone he knew

Drayton R. McQuay, my nephew. Born December 7, 2012, Drayton came into our lives during the darkest hour. He's a light to all around him, and the apple of his father's eye. I love his big, bold personality, and that heartwarming smile.

Otis. W. Hughes, my grandfather. I don't know much about him, but what I do know is this. He was born March 24, 1924 in Raleigh County West Virginia. Though rumor has it he was actually an adopted immigrant. He died when I was two, but inspired me to look into my roots. If I could say anything to him it would be, "Thanks grandpa."

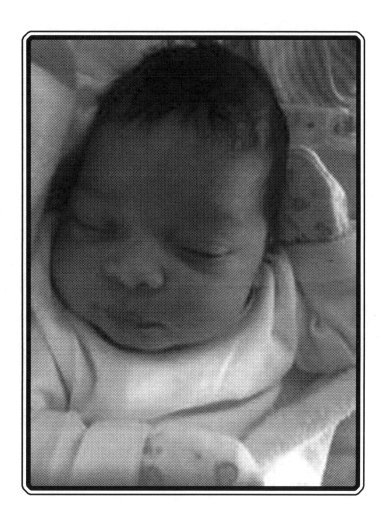

Aaliyah S. Harris, born January 24, 2009

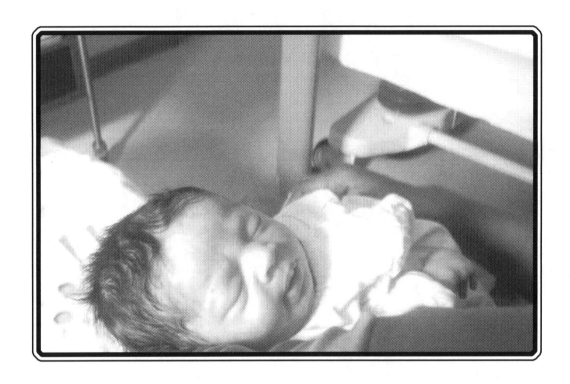

April C. Harris, born June 8, 2010

Me at age 20. Life dealt me a pretty hard hand, at this point, but I was determined not to let it beat me. I've always known greatness lies within me. At the time, I didn't know how to tap int

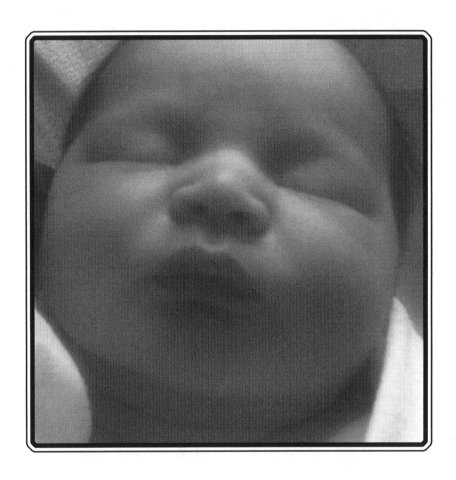

Michael C. Harris III, born June 13, 2016

My father Fredrick L. Hughes. This picture is from his days in
the service. My dad was a member of the airforce.

My husband and I. I can think of no one better to share my life with.
He's my soulmate, the love of my life, and my everything

My mother Shelby J. Hughes. She's a wife, mother of 5, grandmother
of 7 (5 living, and 2 in heaven) and graduate of Kaplan University.
After sacrificing for those she loves, my mother focused o

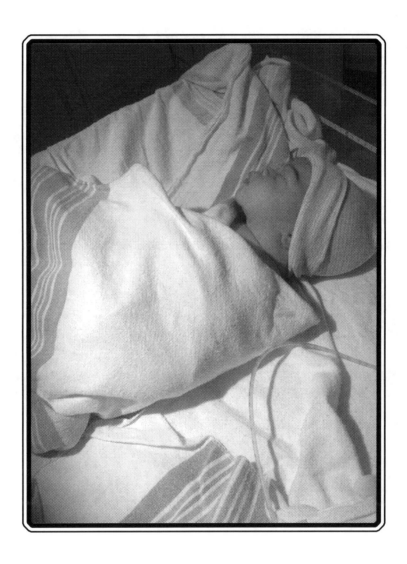

Paris M. Harris, born May 13, 2014

Michael and I on our wedding day. December 23, 2011 I married the love of my life.
The belief in love, or even a soulmate never crossed my mind, then I met this man.

Brothers in arms. My brothers, Anthony and Travis, on duty. I am sure many of you would like to thank them for their service. Absent from my family photos are my brothers, Tiance and Tyrrell.

My mother-in-law and our beautiful daughters.

Thanksgiving 2016, I love playing hostess.

CHAPTER 5

Answering Life Long Questions

In the previous chapter, we discussed the genetic test and how it is used to determine ancestry. When testing my saliva, I found I am 71.1% Sub-Saharan African. Most African Americans are 73.2% African; my report is slightly below average. So where does the rest of my ancestry come from? With all this blood from the "Motherland" you'd think I'd tan a little deeper in the summer, but I don't. Why? Well, it turns out I'm also 27.6% European, with roots in Britain, Ireland, Scandinavia, and the Iberian Peninsula. I've spent years trying to pinpoint the DNA that gave me olive skin. The Iberian Peninsula is made up of Spain and Portugal, along with Iberia. It is close to Italy, Greece, and Balkan, all places I have roots. In fact, 1.4% of my European ancestry comes from there. Still there's more, I am Southeast Asian and Native American, with a small 0.1% of DNA from the Solomon Islands. I've been told I look "exotic", now I know why. Coincidentally, a genetic test couldn't explain 0.3% of my ancestry.

Most people wouldn't care about that small of a percentage, but I'm not most people. Surprisingly, I'm also 78% Neanderthal. Who would have thought? Tons of questions fill in my mind about the Neanderthal DNA. What are they and where do they come from? How accurate is this test? Aren't Neanderthals cave men? As explained, the Neanderthals were ancient humans that lived in, and were named after, Neander Valley, Germany. Ironically, as I looked deeper into my results, I discovered what may have been a flaw. According to my Ancestral Composition Report, there is no traceable German lineage. However, the Neanderthals lived in Neander Valley, Germany. How can this be I am not German, if I am 78% Neanderthal?

Now the question arises, did Neanderthals live, and mate with humans? The answer is yes, and no. Neanderthals lived, matured, and died at the rate as humans. Interbreeding may have occurred, but humans and Neanderthals only rarely produced offspring. I guess this is why I have such a low percentage of Neanderthal genetics. It has been asked whether they (Neanderthals) were human, or some sub homogenous species. Anatomist Herman Schaffhausen studied the remains of a Neanderthal, found in a cave, in Neander Valley, Germany in 1857. What he discovered is the similarities, and differences, between humans and the mysterious being. *"Schaffhausen pored over the fossils, observing their crests and knobs. He noticed the bones had the overall shaped you'd expect from a human skeleton. But some bones had strange features, too. The skullcap, for example, sported a heavy brow ridge, hanging over the eyes like a boney pair of goggles. It was, at once, human and not."* Zimmerman, Carl, "Are Neanderthals Human?" PBS.org. 20, Sep. 12. Web.

CHAPTER 6

I Am Africa

March 2017, I submitted my saliva to be tested. I knew the process would be long, but grew restless waiting for my report. I was testing with company 23andMe, which files results in 4-6 weeks. A month and a half into the wait, I logged into my account looking for answers. An online database held My Ancestral Composition Report. It showed I am 71.1% Sub-Saharan African. More specifically, I'm 65.5% West African, 2.7% Central and South African, and 2.8% Sub-Saharan. As interesting as this is, I decided to dive deeper. I wanted to know who the people stolen from Africa were. I wanted to know about the tribes and their customs. I wrote this chapter with no knowledge of which of the 50+ countries my ancestors came from, but discovered specific links as I did my research. The total population of Africa (Sub-Sahara) is somewhere between 926 million and 2.2 billion. Africa is home to over fifty four countries. Judging by the demographics of people, coupled with the complex genetic system, it is hard to tell which of these countries my ancestors called, "home." To find out who the stolen children of Africa were, I had to turn to other sources. Additionally, Africans often traveled throughout the continent, and likely mixed with differing tribes, in other countries. We also have to take into consideration the African Slave trade, and how slaves were treated. History tells us a slave was the "property" of his or her "master." Said "master" had the ability to do whatever he saw fit with his "property", thus intermixing occurred. The Arab buyers of the African slaves introduced the trade to the Europeans, and thus our ancestors were dragged to America. In school I learned the families were broken apart, in order to prevent tribal traditions from being passed from fathers, to children. The fathers were first sold off, to a separate plantation, while the mothers and children were left behind. African mothers were used as breeding tools, and not allowed to rear their own children. However, those same women were used as "wet" nurses to the slave master's white children. I tell my kids all the time, *"History is full of people doing horrible things to one another,"* This is why. Regarding those accountable, the Arabs and Europeans are only part of the equation. You see, we also know from history that Africans themselves owned slaves, and traded with the Arabians, who then sold them to Europeans.

Before we go into the slave trade let us get discuss the tribes who were stolen. Jon Pennington discusses this in "What Tribe Did Those that Were Part of the Trans- Atlantic Slave Trade Come From?" He states, *"According to DNA analysis that compared samples from African-Americans with samples collected from modern day West Africans, African-American DNA is most likely to share genetic characteristics with the Yoruba, Igbo, and the Brong subgroup of the Akan people."* Pennington, Jon "What Tribe Did Those That Were Part of the Trans-Atlantic Slave Trade Come From," 15, Feb. 2015.quora.com. Web. I began wondering this when I got my test results. Since Africa is a continent, with different countries, and primarily tribal, native people; my ancestors can't be summed up to "African." To label them this way denies their heritage and mine. Since I know I'm West African, more specific Yoruba, Igbo, and Brong of the Akan people, let's get to know more about those tribes. Who are the Yoruba?

The Yoruba people are indigenous to the countries Nigeria and Benin, Africa. The term *"Yoruba"* covers several African tribal groups. When we hear this term, we are referring to the Oyo tribe of North Nigeria; the Ife, Ijesa, Ekiti, and Ondo in the east, and the southern Ijebu and Egba. Dr. Wesley Muhammad, a Historian of Religion and graduate of Morehouse University, wrote about the relation and relationship between Islam, and the Ifa Yoruba religion. In his dissertation he discussed belief that Yoruba people originated in Arabia. *"James Small, African American historian as well as Ifa priest, is above articulating the official, traditional Yoruba view of their origin from Arabia. J.A. Atanda, Nigerian historian from the University of Ibadan, is on the other hand articulating the current scholarly view, which dismisses the traditional view of Arabian origins in the light of some linguistic and archeological data suggesting indigenous African origins. Can the orthodox tradition be reconciled with the data? I believe it can in broad terms though not all Yoruba-speaking groups did not originate in Arabia, but an important (and defining) one did."* Muhammad, Wesley PhD. "Ifa and Islam as Sibling Rivals: The Black Arabian Origins of the Yoruba," academia.edu. 4, Feb. 2013. Web. I've long suspected there was a connection between me, and the Middle East. I guess I've found it in the lineage of my Yoruba ancestors. However, Dr. Muhammad stated not all Yoruba originated in Arabia. The question is which group did? If so, this could be where both my father and I get our Middle Eastern looks from. We cannot discuss the Yoruba people without recognizing their customs and culture. The Yoruba practice a religion called, *Ifa*. What is Ifa, you ask. Awodele Ifayemi explains it this way, *"(The) Ifa Religion is an indigenous, earth centered African spiritual tradition which was conceptualized by the Yoruba people of Nigeria, West Africa. According to oral literature, the practice of Ifa originated as far back as eight thousand years ago. Therefore, the Ifa Religion may indeed be the oldest monotheistic religion in the world."* Ifayemi, Awodele, "Ifa Religion-An African Spiritual Tradition," ilefia.org.Web.

Ifayemi describes the relgion further, *"Ifa Religion is balanced on three legs; Orunmila, Orisa, and the Ancestors. The Supreme Being, Olodumare is without gender and is not an active participant in the affairs of living humans. Olodumare is benevolent, and has provided a Universe with all that is needed for humans to be fulfilled and happy. Ifa is characterized by a deep sense of the interdependence of all life. 'Every life form and element of Nature has an inner soul force-including rivers, rocks, clouds, metals, flowers, thunder, and wind. The natural energies that comprise the Universe are called Orisa. Each Orisa has its own specific function. Humans are in constant communication with Orisa energy, whether we're aware of it or not. Through Ifa, we recognize that our Ancestor spirits are always with us and must be honored, acknowledged, and consulted.'"* Ifayemi, Awodele "Ifa Religion-An African Spiritual Tradition," ileifa.org.Web. Most would find these tradition to be anything from silly to blasphemous, but it depends on the individual, and his or her beliefs. To the Yoruba people, Ifa is as sacred as Christianity is to Christians or Islam to Muslims. Religion isn't the only important aspect of Yoruba culture. There is also marriage, heritage, ritual practices, and art.

The Yoruba people have a very unique approach to marriage. As with most cultures, before there can be a marriage there must be an engagement. However, in Yoruba culture, their engagement isn't the same as ours. Customary to Yoruba values, the groom to be visits the bride to be's family, accompanied by his father and some friends. The purpose is to get to know one another. The groom, his soon to be family, and vice versa. No necessary preparation goes into the Yoruba engagement, although gifts of tubers of yam and bottled wine are exchanged. The bride to be's family hosts a simple meal (mineral water and rice), as the group discusses when the wedding will take place. This isn't far removed from the American tradition of a groom to be asking the father of his love for her hand in marriage. Both show honor and respect to the family of the bride. When we open ourselves to one another, it is often easier to trust those we know, or hope to. Afterwards, invitations are sent, and here comes the bride. This is one of two ceremonies, the first being the "introduction ceremony." The second ceremony, or engagement ceremony is the wedding. "This is when the couple is united together as husband and wife according to Yoruba Culture and Tradition. "As with any other wedding, the occasion is graced with lots of fun, singing, dancing, laughing, blessing the couple, and praying." Yoruba Wedding "The Breakdown of Yoruba Traditional Wedding with pictures and Illustrations." Yorubawedding.com. 2017.Web. A total of 13 steps take place in a traditional Yoruba marriage; 1.)The arrival of the bride's family, 2.)The arrival of the groom's family, 3.) Presentation of Proposal letter from grooms family, 4.) Presentation of acceptance letter from bride's family, 5.) Arrival of the groom, 6.) Arrival of the bride, 7.) Presentation of gifts, 8.) Presentation of rings, 9.) Presentation of the hat, 10.) Introduction of family members, 11.) Cutting the cake, 12.) Presentation of Dowry (Owo ori), and 13.) Prayer for the newest couple from both parents. There you have it, the Yoruba wedding.

As mentioned earlier, some believe the Yoruba originated in Arabia. Dr. Muhammed examined these claims in his dissertation. Muhammad presents two arguments, one stating the Yoruba were Arabian, and the other denying such claims. James Smalls, and J.A. Atanda, present differing points of view, with historical backings, disputing the origin of the Yoruba. *"The Yorubas tell a very interesting story about their origin. They say they came from Saudi Arabia, what is now Saudi Arabia….(In) the early days before the Red Sea expanded to what it is…it was just a trickle river, because the Red Sea is just an expansion of the Rift Gorge…the Rift Valley that runs all the way up to Turkey and starts down below Tanzania. That same valley (is) where most of life found its beginning. That water in the Red Sea has covered up that valley so there's a lot of black bones down there. But this piece of land which is now a desert, but wasn't always desert, that is called Saudi Arabia, if the center of the home of these African peoples who call themselves Yorubas. In ancient times that (area, Saudi Arabia) was… the eastern sector of what we now call Egypt or sometimes Eastern Ethiopia."* James, Baba, Dr. Wesley Muhammad, "Ifa And Islam As Sibling Rivals: The Black Arabian Origins of The Yoruba," 4, Nov. 2013. Academia.edu. Web. Here, James presents a strong argument for the Arabian origins of the Yoruba people. We know Sub-Saharan Africans were a traveling people, but just how far did they go? On the other hand, the counter argument state, *"On the basis of language…the Yoruba people could not have originated from either Arabia, Egypt, or Nubia…the Yoruba language has no family relationship with Arabic, the primary language of the people of Mecca and the rest of Arabia."* Professor J.A. Atanda, Muhammad, Wesley Ph.D. ""Ifa And Islam As Sibling Rivals: The Black Arabian Origins of The Yoruba," 4, Nov. 2013. Academia.edu. Web. The accuracy of Atanda's claims can be backed by scientists findings, through genomes, that African-Americans share the same DNA as Yorubas; the people indigenous to Nigeria.

Yoruba art at its finest can be found by the rivers of Nigeria at the Oshun Oshumobo Grove. The Oshun Oshumobo Grove, home to hundreds of Yoruba gods and goddesses, all of whom help humanity in some way. In a CNN special, "Inside Africa," journalists followed the Nigerian tribe, to the sacred Grove, and was granted access inside Yoruba rituals. Perhaps the most important goddess is the goddess of love and fertility, Oshun. It is said Oshun will supply the needs of the people. In the words of Osafunke Iworo Oshun, Yorbua Traditional Priest, *"When you come here and tell Oshun, 'I am looking for a baby,' you get a baby. 'I'm looking for a husband,' you get a husband. 'I am looking for money,' you get money. Whatever a person asks, Oshun will always give the person, because it is important for the society."* CNN, "Inside Africa: Explore The Culture of The Yoruba," cnn.com.Web. Yoruba religious tradition declares the need to please goddess Oshun with food offerings. As one would feed this wife so she could produce a baby, so do the Yoruba the river, to be blessed by Oshun. The Grove has withstood the test of time, that isn't without conflict. Art activists have fought for the preservation of both the Oshun Oshumbo Grove, and the Yoruba's religious traditions. Although a great many of tribal people are turning away from Ifa, the priestesses still fight to keep tradition alive.

The Ani Igbo (Igboland) is home to the Ndi Igbo people of Africa. These people belong to a community known as Olu no Igbo, meaning *those in the lowlands and uplands.* Prior to European colonialization, the Ndi Igbo lived in non-unified communities. Through expansion, ritual subordination, intermarriage, etc. the unification began. Villages and village groups were identified by the unique, and distinct names of their ancestors; names such as Umuleri or Ezza. As mentioned earlier, studies have indicated African-Americans share DNA with the Yorubas, Ndi Igbos, and Brong peoples of the Akan. Like the Yorubas, the Ndi Igbo can be divided into subgroups, and divided again into individual tribes. The five subcultures are; northern Igbo, southern Igbo, western Igbo, eastern Igbo, and northeastern Igbo. Mistakenly referred to as *Heebo* or *Ebos* (words presumed to be a corruption of Hebrew) the Igbo root *bo* is of Sudanic origin. Not only have I learned I have roots in Nigeria, but now Sudan. The Ndi Igbo also live in and around Nigeria. They also populate a number of diverse countries.I find this interesting. Some scholars believe the root word (*bo*) comes from *gboo*, a word meaning *"to protect,"* or *"to shelter."* Other theorists believe it traces to *Igala*, among word such as *oni* (*the people*) or *onigbo "slave."*

Historically, the Ndi Igbo migrated from overpopulated and less fertile areas, to more prosperous regions. Beginning in 1434 to 1807 the Europeans began making contact with Africans along the Niger coast. Slave trade began in the region leading to the development of states. The Portuguese came to Nigeria, followed by the Dutch and British. The nineteenth century brought Christianity, and colonialism to the region. Onitsha became home to Christian Missionary Society and Catholics missions between 1857 and 1885. Religion plays a pivotal role in any country. Nigeria is no different. Among the waring Christians and Muslims lives a minority of Igbo Jews. These people believe themselves to be the lost tribe of Israel. CNN journalist Chika Oduah interviewed Ndi Igbo Jews on their beliefs. She was told, *"The son of Yakkov, Jacob (was) Gad and I learned he was among one of those people who went out of Israel into exile. So from there he had a son called Eri, and a son gave birth to a son named Aguleri and that's how the Igbo race began."* Oduah, Chika, "Nigeria's Igbo Jews: The 'Lost Tribe' of Israel," CNN. com/news. 4, Feb. 2013. Web. Oral traditions and religious rituals have been passed down from one generation to the next, of Jewish origin. Despite claims of Israeli linkage, some dismiss the Igbo people as Jewish. *"Contemporary views in Igbo scholarship dismiss completely earlier claims of Jewish or Egyptian origin-that is, 'the Hamitic hypothesis'-as the 'oriental mirage.'"* Encyclopedia of World Culture, "Igbo" The Gale Group Inc. encyclopedia.com, 1996. Web. However, as recent as 2013, researchers made the link. Daniel Lis, one of the leading Igbo Jewish identification researchers noted a clear continuity of Jewish identity among Igbos. *"It's not just something that happened yesterday."* Oduah, Chika, "Nigeria's Igbo Jews: The 'Lost Tribe' of Israel," CNN.com/ news. 4, Feb. 2013. If the Jewish traditions are a "continuity," when did they begin? According to the Swiss-Israeli anthropologist, the Jewish identity can be traced back to the 18th century. I find this particularly interesting because we're never told about the Jews of Africa. We know in 70 C.E, the Romans ran the Jews out of Israel. Those peoples scattered to Europe, Russia, the Asias, and (as confirmed) parts of Africa, including Ethiopia.

The Akan total about five to six million people. They're indigenous to Ghana, in constituent kingdoms such as Akeyum, Akwamu, Akuaupem, and Kwahu. The Akan people consist of the Asante (with Ahanta and Wasa) and Anyi. The Anyi cluster something like fifteen kingdoms. Additionally the Attie cluster four kingdoms, the Baule, around seven kingdoms. The Brong, and Fante states also. Historic findings also link these tribes to the Sahara, due to the exchange of gold and salt, by the Akan people. Their cultural traits indicate they may have been successors to Ghana and Mali. The Akan marriage is much easier than the Yoruba. While the Yorubas pay a dowry, and exercise a ritual step of ceremonies, the Akan keep things simple. *"Marriage is expected to be exogamous, and is extremely simple. There is no bride wealth, the union being affected by the transfer of rum or other drink and some money from the groom to the bride's immediate family. Divorce is extremely easy and may be initiated by either men or women. The most usual causes are adultery and barrenness of wives."* Encyclopedia World Culture, "Akan," The Gale Group Inc. encyclopedia. com, 1996. Web. In addition to their easy marriages, their family life was quite unique. As with many communities, and societies, the men lead the people. Children play an important role in Akan legacy, as lineage is passed either to the children of a man's closest sister (mostly her sons), or the children a man has with his wife; when he dies. Akan people owned slaves, and used them for many purposes. Some were taken captive as prisoners of war, criminals, those who opposed local chiefs, or local ritual leaders. Slaves were used for domestic labor, trade, and sacrifices to royal and other ancestors. I knew in writing this chapter I'd have to discuss the Trans-Atlantic Slave Trade. However, I also didn't expect to immediately stumble upon information regarding African people, and their involvement in the capture, and exchange of slaves. The Akan often obtained their slaves from northern Muslims. The notion of slavery is nothing new, in fact, it still exists in parts of Africa, today. What bothers me is when we discuss the Trans-Atlantic slave trade, we do so in a manner that puts all blame for the Slave Trade on just the Europeans. That isn't the entire truth. Don't get me wrong, I'm in no way defending their role in the slave trade, because they were wrong; there's no way to get around it. However, if we're going to discuss the history of the slave trade, let us have all the information, and hold everyone involved equally accountable. The Arab Muslims traded slaves with Africans, who captured and sold their own people as slaves.

Beginning in the 15 century, the African slave trade started with a small amount of people begin taken, and sold as slaves. Due to increasing numbers of plantations in both the Caribbean and America, the demand for slaves grew. African traders captured and sold slaves, sometimes multiple times, before the hostages were introduced to Europeans. Many slaves were brought to the shore from countries nowhere near the sea. It had been the first time they saw the sea, and the first time they saw a white person. Rumors spread that the whites were coming to collect, and eat their captives. Many slaves feared this, and would rather committed suicide than die at the hands of assumed cannibal Europeans. Slaves drawn from the middle of Africa were taken to the coast, from the coast they were forced on ships. Aboard these ships, slaves were taken from West Africa along the Middle Passage, which ended in Europe. Ships carrying firearms, gunpowder, cloth, brandy, and iron headed to the coast of Africa to exchange these goods for human cargo. Along the ships, slaves remained in dungeons for weeks, months and even a year. Slaves were told they were to work fields, but since they'd come accustomed to working crops they knew it didn't take as many as were stolen to complete field work. Something worse was happening, and what is worse is the stolen children of Africa would never make it home to tell what happened. Olaudah Equinao, a slave captures in childhood tells his experiences. *"When I looked round the ship too and saw a large furnace of copper boiling, and a multitude of black people of every description chained together, every one of their countenances expressing dejection and sorrow, so I no longer doubted my fate, and quite overpowering with harrow and anguish. I fell motionless on the deck and fainted...I asked if we were not to be eaten by those white men with horrible looks, red faces and long hair?"* PBS, "The Middle Passage: 1600-1800," pbs.org.Web. I can't imagine the horror my ancestors felt riding the slave ship. They didn't choose to be onboard, they were forced. They were victimized by the African tribes who captured and sold them. Victimized by the Muslims who bought, used, and sold them, and victimized by the Europeans who bought them, chained them, and rewrote their destiny. Some 12.5 million slaves were taken from Africa, an undetermined amount died along the way. Those who grew ill aboard ships were thrown into the sea. I try to imagine the fear of my ancestors who watched helplessly as their brethren were tossed overboard. I know it hurt to watch. It probably hurt worse to want to help, but not be able to. The living quarters on the ships gave barely enough room to turn oneself. The heat of men, women, and children packed on top of one another, like moving boxes, coupled with lack of proper facilities for slaves to use the bathroom, gave rise to perspiration, odor, and the fecal matter bacteria causing sickness. These living conditions, plus the uncertainty of what was to happen, led many slaves to attempt suicide. Some tried to starve themselves, but were force fed using a *speculum orum*. The captain saw this human cargo as a valuable commodity that needed to reach the New World. Any slave who tried to starve him or herself was tortured. If that didn't work, the force fed procedure was instituted.

Jamestown, Virginia 1619 the first slaves reached America. Their purpose, to aid the lucrative production of tobacco crops. African slaves were desired among the European slaveholders, because they were much cheaper, and less costly than the poor, white indentured servants. Slavery, as an economic necessity, was more of a southern system than a northern. In the north, it made very little (if any) sense to own slaves, as the plantations, crops, and business flourished in the south. That isn't to say some northern individuals didn't grow rich from slavery. Though they didn't hold slaves in their homes, they did invest in both the Trans-Atlantic slave trade, and southern plantations. However, the 18ᵗʰ century brought the exhaustion of the land used to grow tobacco. Southern states faced and economic crisis, but slavery continued to grow in America. The development of the cotton gin, a machine Eli Whitley created, aided in the production of cotton; which needed to have its seeds removed. Until the invention of the cotton gin, slaves were required to remove cotton seeds by hand. Eli's invention was both copied and spread throughout the south. The new invention led to a switch in southern states, but only reinforced those states need for slave labor. Westward expansion and a growing abolitionist movement led to the great debate over the necessity of slavery. Northern religious peoples argued it unethical because they believed it to be sinful. Other, non-religious peoples argued it was regressive, inefficient, and made little economic sense. Free northern blacks, and some white northerners, organized a system of freeing southern slaves. The most popular method was hiding slaves in safe houses along the Underground Railroad. The U.S. Constitution acknowledged the institution (slavery), even counting slaves as three-fifths of a person, specifically for taxation reasons. The amendment also stated the right to repossess any person held to service or labor. We know from early childhood education, a slave was seen as property, nothing more. While slaves were not legally bound in marriage, some did marry and create families. Slave owners often encouraged this practice, but quickly sold family members to separate plantations. The division of the family hurt the slave further. Slave owners were permitted to do as pleased with their human "property." Slave rape, and the production of bi-racial slave children resulted. A division was created among slaves, by complexion and status as workers (i.e. house slaves or house Negros and field slaves or field Negros.) The division was created to prevent unity among slaves making them easy to control. Slave owners feared nothing more than a slave revolt, and no rebellious slave more than Nat Turner. Nat Turner led a revolt with the aid of 75 slaves, who conquered 60 whites, before leading to his capture and death.

Conflict over slavery and its possible future expansion or limitation rose during the westward expansion. The 1820 debate over government rights to restrict a newly developing state's (Missouri) application for statehood reached a compromise. Missouri would be admitted as a slave state, while Maine a free state. This act became known as the Missouri Compromise. The 1854 Kansas-Nebraska Act asserted the rule of popular sovereignty and opened new territories to slavery. 1857 brought the ruling of the Dred Scott case, a case of a slave who sued for his freedom, arguing he'd been brought into a free state as a slave. The Supreme Court eventually ruled all territories were open to slavery. John Brown's actions at Harpers Ferry, Virginia in 1859 led to further tensions. The executed Brown was considered a martyred hero by abolitionists, and a murdering thug by southerners. The following year led to the rise of Republican presidential candidate Abraham Lincoln. Lincoln's antislavery views were well established, but the Union wasn't aiming to end slavery during the Civil War; not at first. The original intent was to preserve America as a nation, slavery became an aim later. January 1, 1863 President Abraham Lincoln signed the Emancipation Proclamation stating, *"Slaves within any state, or designed part of a State...in rebellion, shall be then, thenceforward, and forever free."* History Channel, "Slavery In America," History.com. Web.

CHAPTER 7

I Am Europe

In the previous chapter, we discovered my African roots. As noted, I'm not entirely African, so we continue to the next land of my origin, Europe. I guess it came as no surprise that I have European ancestry. The blue eyes and the production of have been traced to Europe. According to my Ancestral Composition Report, I am 21.9% Northern European. This is broken down to 6.2% British and Irish, 0.9% Scandinavian. We know Scandinavia is made up of the countries Norway, Denmark, and Turkey. I am also 14.9% Broadly Northern European, 2.2% Southern Europe. To be specific, 0.7% Iberian and 1.4% Broadly Southern European. I'm also 3.5% Broadly European, so my ancestors here could come from anywhere. The one thing I can't figure is why no link to Germany was found. My maiden name Hughes, is of German origin. Knowing this, I have to take into consideration that many of my ancestors, on both sides, were slaves. Slaves were bought and sold in America, like they were in Africa. Once a slave was "purchased," the slave owner changed the name of the person, giving his "new property" his own last name. It is why we (in America) have so many African descendants with European names.

We're all familiar with the 1492 voyage of Christopher Columbus to India. However, we are not as familiar with the 1492 exile of Sephardic Jews from Spain. This part of history is particularly interesting to me, because I have lineage in Spain. One must wonder if I'm a little Jewish. Before we get to the exile, we should know how the Jews came to the Iberian Peninsula. There's no clear concise evidence to explain the early Jews arrival in the Iberian Peninsula. In fact, it is highly speculated that they migrated to the region with the Romans under the Roman Empire. However, evidence does exist to show their early existence in the region. Some Jewish myths exist to explain their residency. Some believe King Solomon sent his men to collect tax monies from the western corner of the Mediterranean, and that is how the Jews came to be in the area. Others believe their communities existed in the peninsula centuries prior to the Roman Empire, as far back as the beginning of human existence. A people liken themselves unto the region, not as immigrants or new comers, but as natural citizens. The grave of a one year old, Anna

Solomon Ulla, engraved with Latin inscriptions, proves their early existence to the peninsula. The New Testament tells of the Apostle Paul and his venture to Spain. Paul is a biblical follower of Christ, who after Jesus's crucifixion, began to spread the gospel. He is known to visit areas with Jewish populations, to try and sway non-believers to Christianity. This was during the first century. However, the first official evidence of a large Jewish population, in the Iberian Peninsula, is given in the fourth century. During this time Christianity became the main religion under Roman rule. Emperor Constantine's conversion pushed the popularity of the gospel.

To further prove the existence of Jews in the Iberian Peninsula, we look at the Roman council legislation. Of the many edicts written, four specifically apply to the Jews. The first of these reads, *"If heretics should refuse to cross over to the Catholic Church, Catholic maidens shall not be given unto them."* A heretic is any Christian who does not follow what is believed to be ideas, and values, of Christianity. Continuing, *"It was resolved to give them neither to Jews, because no association could exist between the faithful, and the infidel."* Benjamin R. Gampel, "From Golden Age To Expulsion: History, Society, and Culture of Medieval Sephardic Jewry Part 1a," YouTube.com. 28, Nov. 2011. Web. We can safely assume, from this law, that Catholic girls were marrying Jewish guys. While the law forbids the marrying of Catholic girls to Jewish men, it says nothing about Jewish women to Catholic men. Why is this? Could it be that women were subsumed into the religious beliefs of their husbands? Edict two and three read, *"It was resolved to warn the landowners, that they should not suffer that their fruits which they received with Thanksgiving from God shall be blessed by Jews, lest they make our blessing null, and void. If anyone should unlawfully presume to do so, subsequent to this interdiction, he shall be utterly expelled from the church." "It is resolved that if parents should act contrary to this interdiction, they shall be removed for five years."* Benjamin R. Gampel, "From Golden Age To Expulsion: History, Society, and Culture of Medieval Sephardic Jewry Part 1a," YouTube.com. 28, Nov. 2011. Web From this we know Christian owned crops were blessed by the Jews. Had it not been so, there would've been no need for this law. Marrying your Catholic daughter to a Jewish man resulted in a five year ban. Lastly, edict four, *"If one of the faithful with a wife should commit adultery with a Jewess or with a Gentile, he shall be kept away from communion. If he should be exposed by another man, he shall be allowed to join the Lord's communion when he has completed a five year penance."* Benjamin R. Gampel, "From Golden Age To Expulsion: History, Society, and Culture of Medieval Sephardic Jewry Part 1a," YouTube. com. 28, Nov. 2011. Web. Adultery, in Christianity, is a sin. No matter whom the adulterer is, he or she commits and act, forbidden by God, when having an extramarital affair. However, it goes further than this. Any child conceived, during an extramarital affair, was lawfully reared by the mother. If she was Jewish, or pagan, that child was rejected by the Catholic Church. The law was created to prevent lost children from being reared into paganism or as Jews. Since laws were enacted to keep separation between Christians and Jews, we must know there were mutual relationships the Catholic Church found threatening. After all, it takes two to tango.

The year 476 brought an end to the Roman Empire. The Germanic tribes which once patrolled the northern boarders, in an era of political and military decline, we conquered Rome. The 5th century saw many battles between the Romans and Germanic tribes, also known as the Visigoths. The once powerful Roman Empire was split between its former allies in 476. The Visigoths saw no reason to keep Roman Empire pretenses, because they represented the true energy and force behind the Empire. Shortly after, the Visigoths conquered the Iberian Peninsula. Their time of rule begun with a light, but adopted both Roman law and Legislation. True to people everywhere, the Visigoths were religious. They practiced a form of Christianity called Arianism. Unlike its Catholic counterpart, Aryan Christianity focused on the trinity, not divinity, of Jesus. However, they also focused more the humanity of Christ. Still the Visigoths didn't see much difference between themselves and the Jews. They happily took over Roman Legislation and laws which affected Jews, but a change was coming. In 586, the Aryans were ruled by a new king, Rakha. A change of religion caused a rise in discrimination of Jews. King Rakha converted from Visigothic Arianism to Catholicism. Sisebut came to power in 612, and issued a shocking edict. Under his rule, Sisebut ordered all Jews to be forcibly converted to Christianity. The forced conversion made no sense. Forced conversion was forbidden by the Catholic Church. Economically it made no sense, and it wasn't reasonable to force a well-integrated part of the population to convert. However, under the rule of the following king, the Jewish, Christian converts were allowed (slowly) to return to their religion. This is the first of three times Jews were forced to convert. The last, and final forced conversion happened in 1492, under Spain's leadership. The launch of the Inquisitions inspired the signing of the *Alhambra Decree*. Accusations flew of Jews trying to turn Christians to their "wicked" practices. *"In 1492, as every American schoolchild knows, King Ferdinand and Queen Isabella of Spain sent Christopher Columbus on a fateful voyage to India that ended up changing the history of the world. But 1492 was also as a dolorous year in the history of European Jewry. On March 31, 1492, Spain's hard-line Catholic rulers issued a decree offering Jews in the country a terrible choice: Convert to Christianity or get out. Many fled, giving rise to a worldwide diaspora of 'Sephardic' Jews, after the Hebrew word for Spain."* Henry Chu, "Welcome Home, 500 Years Later: Spain Offers Citizenship to Sephardic Jews," latimes.com 1, Oct. 2005. Web.

Great Britain, or more specifically The United Kingdom of Great Britain and North Ireland is a constitutional monarchy. Divided into two segments, Great Britain consists of England, Wales, and Scotland. The total population, as of 2011, is 63,181,775 with 94,226 square miles. The United Kingdom rests on the island Ireland, in the Irish Sea and Channel Islands. I am surprised (not really) to know part of my heritage comes from this region. What does Europe contribute to who I am? The horrific treatment of the Sephardic Jews is only a part of the history of Europe. When examining the past, we must accept the bad, while acknowledging the good. Let us continue. Great Britain was formed in 1707 with the Act of Union, between Scotland and England. Prior to this, Great Britain dealt primarily with England. When Britain was established, English history became part of its own. Today, it is the fourth most populous country in Europe. The 1701 *Act of Settlement* laid the ground rules of British royalty. Just what is the Act of Settlement? The fleeing of King James II in 1688 during the "Glorious Revolution" left an empty throne. His beliefs in the right of the Crown and Catholic sympathies gave way for parliamentarians to offer the thrown to his daughter, Mary. She accepted on one condition; she would be allowed to reign with her Dutch husband, William of Orange (William III). So what exactly did the Act of Settlement do? *"The Act of Settlement of 1701 was designed to secure the Protestant succession to the throne, and to strengthen the guarantees for ensuring a parliamentary system of government."* "The Act of Settlement" royal.uk. Prior to the Act, the Bill of Rights was set in motion establishing the order of succession for Mary's heirs. The Bill of Rights, under the Act of Settlement, was reinforced in strengthening government principal that was undertaken by the Sovereign and his constitutional advisors. Problems regarding the throne arose beginning in 1694. The throne was to be succeeded by the heirs of Mary II, however she died in 1694 of smallpox, aged 32; leaving no heirs. William III grew ill by 1700 and Queen Anne's only child, Duke of Gloucester, died at 11. This lead to the decision by Parliament that all future successors should be Protestant.

Between 2,200-2,500 years ago, out of the European arc, tiny movements began taking place. These movements would later go further to produce Hinduism and Jainism, in the Indus Valley. Writers, west in Europe, began recording the works of a new religion, Druidism. Although not certain, it is argued Druidism was in existence longer than what is known. In 50 CE Julius Cesare wrote Druidism originated in Britain, but its first works were noted in year 200 BCE in Greece. Some believe Druids stretch from every corner of Europe, but scholars deny these claims. In fact, they say it is unlikely so; rather Druids were native to the British Isles, Western Gaul (France), and Ireland. Further speculation believes Druidism, and its magical practices evolved out of a pre-Druidic cult, before becoming a religion. *"The evidence of the religious activities of the prehistoric inhabitants of western Europe is remarkable: on the Gower Peninsula, near Swansea in Wales, Paviland caves have revealed one of the earliest magico-religious sites in the world, where around 26,000 years ago a group of humans carefully interred a skeleton wrapping the body in cloth or rubbing it with red ochre and laying it with mammoth-ivory rods, which may be the earliest magic wands ever found."* The Order of Bards Ovates & Druids, "A Long History of Druidry," druidry. org. 26, Aug. 2017. Web. If Druidism grew out of a pre-Druidic cult, where did this other religion come from, and who inspired it? 17,000 year old cave inscriptions of animal paintings rest in the Lascaux caves in France. These paintings are said to be the works of Druids. What evidence exists to prove this, Druid cave meetings. Today, animal inscriptions play a major part in the new, and growing, Druid movement. The cave is symbolic of the womb. Well, what comes from the womb, but new life? It makes sense that a movement in need of a comeback would pick something similar to a womb from which to be reborn. The recent rise of Druidry sounds interesting, but what do we know of its past?

Druids were more than just religious magicians. They had a hand in all professions, and sought knowledge wherever they could find it. Druids held positions of judges, poets, historians, and physicians. The Druids covered every part of Ireland, Tara, Irelands resident over-king, earned the reputation as *"chief seat of idolatry and druidism of Erin."* Necromantic powers attributed to Druids include the production of madness. Madness was believed to be brought on by magical incantations, rather than chemical imbalances in the brain as we know now. For this reason, the *"madman's wisp"* was created. Druids formed the wisp from straw or grass. Incantations were said over the wisp, and flung into the faces of a victim; allegedly causing the victim to go insane or idiotic. *"Madness was often produced by the rage of battle. For, during a bloody battle, it sometimes happened that an excitable combatant ran mad with fury and horror: and occurrences of this are recorded in the romantic accounts of nearly all great battles fought in Ireland."* Library Ireland: Irish books online, "A Smaller Social History of Ancient Ireland," libraryireland.com.1906.Web. Madness causing spells aren't the only aspect of Druidism. Much like any religion, rituals play an important role in its practices. The Imbolc Rite, a ritual honoring goddess Brighid, is among many important Druidic rituals. How do the Druids carry out this practice? Religious rituals occur at all times throughout the year. Passover for the Jews, takes place in spring. It is a sacred feast that takes place to honor the Jewish exit from Egypt. Likewise Christians honor the birth of Jesus Christ, on Christmas; and celebrate his resurrection in the spring around Easter. Muslims holy Ramadan takes place during the summer. It is a time of spiritual cleansing. So the Druidic Imbolc Rite, a winter ritual, isn't so strange. It is believed that Brighid's face is hardened until the winter solstice. At this time she wears the face of "the Hag." Winds become bitter at the sight of this face, and plants die. However, on the eve of Imbolc, sheep's lactate, producing fresh milk, and the goddess transforms into a young maiden. The Druidic people call this time of change *"January Thaw."* Young girls play an important role in the Imbolc Rite. My guess is the goddess is most appeased by the leadership of young women. Talk about girl power. Together, young girls gather and to make a "Bride Doll." The doll is created from straw, grains, or reeds of the previous year's harvest. It (the doll) is dressed in finery and placed in a basket with a white rod, a "slanchdan" of birch, willow, bramble, or broom; all symbolic to the "magic-wand" and Brighid's weather controlling ability.

As the children busy themselves adult bake sweet cakes and ready dairy foods to honor the festival. Armed solar crosses are plaited, made of reed and straw, "to hasten" the strength of the sun. Still more work is done, as young girls form a procession and march outside three times, likely under direction of the sun; white candle in hand, accompanied with the Bride Doll. The girls make their way around their respective village, blessing the homes of all, as they go from door to door. Each speaking this blessing, *"We ask that Brighid bless this household, all herein and their kindred and their substance."* Order of White Oak: Ord Na Darach Gile "Imbolc Rite: A Feast for Girls," whiteoakdruids.org. 1999. Web. Each household gives a girl a small gift and a sweet cake. Lastly, the girls stop at the home of a prepared party. Each brings snowdrops or other flowers to the host's house and blesses the home. In return, the host welcomes the children with, "In this house you girls are the personification of the Goddess and of the Land. You do us honor by your presence here. Welcome in and accept our hospitality." Order of White Oak: Ord Na Darach Gile "Imbolc Rite: A Feast for Girls, "whiteoakdruids.org. 1999. Web. Growing up Baptist, I was taught all other religions, and their practices were *"evil."* I'm not sure I believe that anymore. It is human nature to fear what we don't understand. So it is practical to assume rituals, such as the Imbolc Rite, were feared by non-Druidic people. The belief in many gods, or even in goddesses, is farfetched for some, but to the Druids it is sacred. Baby blessings, similar to a Catholic Christening, are another common Druidic ritual. In a Catholic Christening, the child is confirmed, and baptized, by his or her priest. The Druid Baby Blessing Ritual follows similar protocol, but without the water. Druids dress their child(ren) in a beautiful garment, much like a Christening gown, of a Catholic. The family stands before an indoor altar, topped with a candle (triple wicked) and a bowl of sacred water. Does this sacred water sound familiar? If not, it should. Holy water is as familiar to Catholicism, and sacred water to Druids. There the similarities end. In a Catholic Christening, the child is baptized, by way of water. The Druidic practice doesn't require the child to get wet. As a priest says a holy blessing over a newly baptized baby, the Druidic officiant chants a blessing over the child. I'm sure there's more to the Druidic religion than what I've stated, here. However, time doesn't warrant me to dive too deep into its practice, history, etc. My journey started with a lot of curiosity and the more I learn, the better I am able to accept, and understand me. Knowing my African and European roots helped me to come to terms with the struggle of racial identity. I was born of black parents, but as I look in the mirror I cannot deny what I see; I see the mix of nations staring back at me. I have the red skin of Natives; eyes as blue as the sea, I inherited from Europeans. My hair defies gravity to kiss the sky above. I now see traces of lineage I didn't notice before. What hasn't shown in me was passed to my four children. Let us continue.

CHAPTER 8

I Am Oceania, Southeast Asia, and Indigenous America

January 2009, during a harsh winter blizzard, I gave birth to a beautiful baby girl. Weighing 6lbs. 3oz., at 19 inches long she changed the path of my destiny. While this sounds beautiful, and it is, I also have a funny story to tell. Our oldest daughter Aaliyah was born at 5:37 p.m. After 19 1/2 hours of labor, I was happy to hold her, touch her, and meet her. Those first moments were precious, but before long she was whisked away to the nursery, and I to recovery. Before the night was over a nurse came to see me. She'd come to do a routine checkup and see if I wanted my baby. Of course I did. Away the nurse went to fetch my darling. Five minutes later she wheeled in a tiny incubator, with a beautiful baby inside. *"Here she is,"* sang the sweet lady. I stretched out my arms to receive the child she extended to me, and I held her. But something wasn't right. I looked down to see an almond eyed, beige skinned, straight haired baby. I started to panic. *"Oh, what a cute baby,"* I began, *"but where's mine?"* There was no possible way this child was mine. I, a black woman, couldn't be the mother of this Asian kid, unless she had an Asian father. My husband isn't oriental, so this must be a mistake. It wasn't. What I didn't see in the delivery room was the nurse attach a bracelet to her ankle with the same number as the one on mine. She was ours alright, but why did she look the way she did? Turns out, she and I both a part Asian. Yes, we're from a little bit of everywhere. Southeast Asia is comprised of eleven countries; in no particular order they are, Indonesia, Thailand, Vietnam, Singapore, Malaysia, Philippines, Cambodia, Myanmar (Burma), Laos, Brunei, and Timor-Leste. In chapter 4 we discovered DNA can go generations before showing up. Our eldest Aaliyah was born looking more like the people of Asia, than those of Africa. Still, she is a mix of the two. She and I carry these genes, as do her two little sisters, and baby brother. However, if you were to come see our kids, you'd see siblings, identical to one another, wearing the genetics of various populations across the world. Proof that God exists, in my book.

The Southeast Asian mainland is a melting pot of religions. It is home to believers of Christianity, Hinduism, Daoism, Islam, and Confucianism, among others. This region is divided into countries Burma, Thailand, Cambodia, Vietnam, and Laos; home to a diverse population of autochthonous tribal religions mingled with Hinduism. Underneath the hotbed of religious diversity lives the prehistoric roots of Southeast Asia. *"Although certain beliefs and practices can be seen as linking peoples of the present to ancient Southeast Asian religions, they have often been reformulated to make since within worldview shaped by historic religions. The processes of religious change have, moreover, intensified in the wake of radical shaking of traditional order taking place throughout the twentieth century."* Encyclopedia of Religion, "Southeast Asia Religions: Mainland Cultures," encyclopedia.com. 2005. Web. What history are my people trying to link themselves to? Southeast Asia's mainland has been in existence as long as the *Homo sapiens*. Evidence further shows this region was home to *Homo erectus*, as well as some other hominoid forms. The birthplace of human life is subject to criticism and interest. I've been told life started in Africa, read the oldest human skulls was found in Ethiopia; but in recent years bible believers flood the internet with tons of evidence of mankind's Iranian origins, in the *Garden of Eden*. Could it be Southeast Asia's mainland was home to the first humans? Whether it is or isn't, Southeast Asia's history is a part of mine. In small percentages, I am connected with the Negrito people, the remaining hunter-gathering groups, and the belief in both spiritual and material quality of rice. Yes, rice; to us it is food, nothing more, but to my ancestors rice is associated with feminine deity. Religion has played a big part in my upbringing, so I find the personification of non-living things, as god or connected to some spiritual being, to be fascinating. Seeing the universal force of God through the eyes of differing groups intensifies my faith; knowing we're all aware of a higher power, in some way.

From the religious diversity of Southeast Asia, to the thousand or so islands of the Pacific, I dig to find more. The Polynesians culture developed in Australia and Oceania, when Southeast Asian sailors explored the South Pacific. Moving east, in 1500 BCE, sailors left New Guinea in double hulled vessels known as outrigger canoes. These canoes could be maneuvered easily, and sail quickly. Polynesians developed a unique navigation system which involved keeping of bird flight patterns, and star and ocean swells observation. Through the domestication and transportation of animals and plants, the Polynesians were able to secure stable and permanent communities in the South Pacific. I've always considered myself crafty and self-reliant, I guess it is an inherited ability. Maybe this is where it comes from. By nature, it seems, I am a survivor. The islands of Melanesia, Micronesia, and Polynesia were colonized by 1000 CE. Less than 1% of my genetic makeup comes from this region, but I believe every bit counts. This journey wouldn't be complete if I forsake the smallest bit of heritage. I want to know as much as I can about every society that blends to make me. Polynesians brought agriculture to the region, even clearing New Zealand's forest by half, with controlled fires. Habitat destruction resulted in a temporary extinction of 40 species of birds. Entire villages were fed on the Giant Moa bird. A large animal, unable to fly, the Moa was an easy hunting target. The Maori disguarded much of the bird's weight as "useless" or "undesirable." More than 1400 birds became extinct as a result. The environment affected the traditional practices of the Australian Aborigine. Myths were developed to explain thing such as the landscape. According to the Aborigine, Australia's coastline was closer to the Barrier Reef. Geologists confirmed this myth. *"During the last glacial period, when sea levels were lower, Australia's coastline did extend kilometers into what is now the ocean."* National Geographic "Australia and Oceania: Human Geography," nationalgeography.org. Web. Some such myths include the belief that the earth's surface was once nothing, but an expanse of clay or mud. Ancestral beings descending from the sky, or rising from under the surface, caused the landscape to change. These beings took the forms of animals, plants, and humans. Now human, the ancestral beings moved across the earth, changing its shape by molding rivers, islands, etc. from mud. They gave birth to living beings and gave humans the gifts of language, belief, and knowledge. The birth of mankind is widely debated. Some believe God put us here, others believe alien beings created us. The Aborigine believe they are the descendants of spirit beings who formed the earth. The importance of ancestral journey to creation is traced in a Songline.

Genesis 1:1 *"In the beginning, God created the heaven and the earth."* Authorized King James Version Holy Bible. Thomas Nelson Bibles. 2003. God, the most universally diverse being ever known. Who is this "God," and where did he come from? Are there many gods or is there only one? Various religions believe different things, but if you ask the Natives you'll find there are quite a few. The polytheistic view of "god" is a worldwide phenomenon. Greeks, Hindus, and Egyptians all left marks on history books with the belief of several gods and goddesses. Different tribes recognize different gods, Anguta, Aninigan, and Idlrvirisissong are deities known to the Inuit/Eskimo tribe. Just who are these beings? Anguta is the collector god of the dead. He carries the deceased, from the earth, to the underworld, where they must spend one year with him. Aninigan, the moon god, is brother to the sun god. He resides in an igloo in the sky. Moon is cousin to Idlrvirisissong, the tricky demon in the sky. Sometimes he appears to dance and entertain. Sounds harmless, right? Wrong, according to Inuit belief, Idlrvirisissong eats the intestines of nearby people who cannot restrain themselves. According to the Cherokee tribe, the sun is a goddess saddened by the kidnapping of her daughter. In her grief, she hid her face, causing darkness to fall upon the earth. It was the Cherokee people, and their gift of song, that healed her sorrow. Southeastern tribal Natives believe trickster god Rabbit, brought fire to man. Faith and spirituality have long withstood the test of time. I see separate views of god(s) and goddesses from one people to another, connected through me. In this most interesting discovery, I found spirituality didn't begin with my Christian upbringing. Likewise, neither did the strength to persevere. 23,000 years ago, the Native Americans migrated to North America. They brought with them a rich culture and beautiful traditions. I would love to retell the story of a wonderful new relationship between the Natives, and European settlers, who made their way to America beginning in 1492, but I can't. The Natives faced some of the harshest forms of discrimination. The Indian Removal Act of 1830, prompted for by Andrew Jackson, forced Natives to relocate. The first Thanksgiving was followed by a horrific massacre, and treaties were formed, yet broken. Natives survived the Trail of Tears, the rape and slaughter of their women and children, all to come to account to about 2% of today's population. Still, the will to persevere lives within them, and within me. I've learned from research that I am, not only the sum of my ancestors' DNA, but the sum of their strength and will to overcome. Whether they were exiled Jews from Spain, enslaved Igbo and Yoruba from Africa, or Natives forced off their land; we've all overcome, we've all persevered, we've all survived.

CHAPTER 9

A New Journey

Now that I have a deeper understanding of who I am the question remains, *what's next?* I started my search knowing nothing about my past. All I knew was my paternal grandfather may have been an immigrant. I never met him, Otis W. Hughes died when I was two. What I had wasn't much, but it was enough to kick start my journey to self-discovery. However, I found myself searching less for answers about Otis's past. I personalized my journey. I wanted to make this about me specifically. Knowing Otis's citizenship status would benefit him none, now. He's gone. Through the genetic testing process I was able to discover I am much more than who I thought I was. Regarding nationality, I am American. What I wasn't sure of was my tribal roots. I had no idea the beautiful, yet misunderstood culture of the Igbo, Akan, and Yoruba is mine. My Irish roots stand firm in the practice of Druidic rituals, and I'm happy to know that five hundred years later; exiled Jews can return to Spain. Still there's more to come. What I know now is the lands my ancestors called "home." I need to know who they are. Putting names to faces will help me understand. It is my dream to travel the globe as I learn about my ancestors. I want to walk where they walked, experience our culture firsthand, and expand my mind. If knowledge is power I now hold the key to being all powerful. My greatest hope is to achieve something meaningful, something not easily obtained, but valued.

A few years ago I started building a family tree. It hasn't been easy. I've had an especially difficult time connecting myself to relatives I've never known. Those I do know are more strangers than family. Still, I started building. At the time I had no clue what I was looking for, but I do now. I believe in destiny and that I will find mine in connecting to my ancestors, learning their stories, and learning from their mistakes. I don't know if you believe in premonitions or prophecies, but I do. I believe it was written, by God, that I should find something out about my heritage, use it, and become great. At age seven I felt my life will carry me to Africa. For what purpose, only God knows. There's no escaping destiny. In the right time, at the right place, I will know what my life's purpose is. Until then, I'll continue building. This book, though informative, was only the first step. I have many more to take. I'm not sure what to expect, but I'm ready for it. Years of questioning my lineage have come to this. I now know where it is I'm from, and that is pretty much everywhere. There's a little bit of all of humanity in me. So what's next? I want to know those overseas strangers like me. I want to know what it is about culture and heritage that makes a person proud. I want to walk in the wisdom of my ancestors. I may push the envelope a little, on things I don't agree with, but that's part of me. I will ask questions and listen when necessary, but also speak my mind. I titled this book, *"Do You Know Who You Are,"* in order to encourage you, the reader, to get to know yourself. You are more than just a face in a crowd. We're all here for a reason, none of us come to be by accident. However, I believe it is up to us to find our life's meaning, and we can do that in understanding the past. My mother used to tell me, *"You'll never know where you're going unless you know where you've been."* This is true. Understanding *"where"* we've been enables us to take control over our lives. We learn so much from our past including *"who"* we are as individuals, and as a people. Be what we may; black and white are colors, not cultures. Human identity is much more complex and beautiful than that. Bearing vague descriptions only identifies what is on the surface. What about the layers beneath? A lot of talk about *"racial pride"* flows in American society, but how can we take pride in something scientists argue is a construct? Do we ignore the facts and carry on blind? Or do we pause and think, *"there's more to me than this."* I've given both sides of the "race" argument in chapter 2, but it isn't my choice to make. Only you can decide what you believe. As for me, I'm well aware I'm more than a ranking on a hierarchy. I know where I've been, and am prepared to go back, learn (again), and reflect. To answer my own question, yes. I know who I am.

Bibliography:

Danielle Dondanville, *"Eye Color, Hair Color, Bloody Types, and Other Traits,"* The Tech Museum of Innovation. Web. 6 December 2016.

Dr. Barry Star, *"Eye Color, Hair Color, Blood Types, and Other Traits"* The Tech Museum of Innovations. Web 3, Dec. 2014.

U.S. National Library of Medicine *OCA2 Melanosomal Transmembrane Protein*, Web. 19, July 2017.

Mornings, Ann "Does Genomes Challenge the Social Construction of Race," Sociological Theory 2014. *DAI* 32:189.

Wade, Nicholas "What Science Says About Race and Genetics," Time.com. 09, May 2014. Web.

Howard, Jacqueline What Scientists Mean When They Say Race Is Not Genetic. Huffington Post, 09, Feb. 2016. Web.

Lawson, William "Anthropologists Disagree About Race and Bones" ABCNews.com. Cable News Network, 06 Oct. 2000.Web.

Omi, Michael, Howard Winant, "Race Formation in the United States: From the 1960s to the 1990s," 2nd Ed. New York; Routledge, 1994. Print.

Lizzie Wade "Genetics Study Reveals Surprising Ancestry of Many American," Sciencemag.org. 18, Dec. 2014.

Bryner, Jeanna. "One Common Ancestor Behind Blue Eyes," LiveScience.com 31, Jan. 2008. Web

Merriam-webster.com/dictionary/haplotypes

O'Hanlon, Leslie "Tracing Your Ancestry," technologyreviews.com 24, Feb. 2006. Web.

23 And Me "How Your DNA Becomes A Report," 23andme.com. 2017.Web.

Zimmerman, Carl, "Are Neanderthals Human?" PBS.org. 20, Sep. 12. Web.

Pennington, Jon "What Tribe Did Those That Were Part of the Trans-Atlantic Slave Trade Come From," 15, Feb. 2015.quora.com. Web.

Muhammad, Wesley PhD. "Ifa and Islam as Sibling Rivals: The Black Arabian Origins of the Yoruba," academia.edu. 4, Feb. 2013. Web.

Ifayemi, Awodele, "Ifa Religion-An African Spiritual Tradition," ilefia.org.Web.

Yoruba Wedding "The Breakdown of Yoruba Traditional Wedding with pictures and Illustrations." Yorubawedding.com. 2017.Web.

Professor J.A. Atanda, Muhammad, Wesley Ph.D. ""Ifa And Islam As Sibling Rivals: The Black Arabian Origins of The Yoruba," 4, Nov. 2013. Academia.edu. Web.

CNN, "Inside Africa: Explore The Culture of The Yoruba," cnn.com.Web

Oduah, Chika, "Nigeria's Igbo Jews: The 'Lost Tribe' of Israel," CNN.com/news. 4, Feb. 2013. Web.

Encyclopedia of World Culture, "Igbo" The Gale Group Inc. encyclopedia.com, 1996. Web

Encyclopedia World Culture, "Akan," The Gale Group Inc. encyclopedia.com, 1996. Web

PBS, "The Middle Passage: 1600-1800," pbs.org.Web.

History, "Slavery In America," History.com. Web.

Benjamin R. Gampel, "From Golden Age To Expulsion: History, Society, and Culture of Medieval Sephardic Jewry Part 1a," YouTube.com. 28, Nov. 2011. Web

Henry Chu, "Welcome Home, 500 Years Later: Spain Offers Citizenship to Sephardic Jews," latimes.com 1, Oct. 2005. Web

"The Act of Settlement" royal.uk

The Order of Bards Ovates & Druids, "A Long History of Druidry," druidry.org. 26, Aug. 2017. Web.

Library Ireland: Irish books online, "A Smaller Social History of Ancient Ireland," libraryireland.com.1906.Web

Order of White Oak: Ord Na Darach Gile "Imbolc Rite: A Feast for Girls," whiteoakdruids.org. 1999. Web

Encyclopedia of Religion, "Southeast Asia Religions: Mainland Cultures," encyclopedia.com. 2005. Web.

National Geographic "Australia and Oceania: Human Geography," nationalgeography.org. Web

Authorized King James Version Holy Bible. Thomas Nelson Bibles. 2003.

About the Author

Author of "Do You Know Who You Are?" Tiffany Harris delivers an eye opener in her book. The twenty eight year old digs into her lineage to uncover what she's never known. The details of her ancestry. Tiffany is a resident of Charleston West Virginia. She lives with her husband and four children, three girls and a boy. Her hobbies include reading, writing (of course) and physical exercise. She is most interested in human history, tradition, culture, and ritual practices. Tiffany operates her own website (tiffanysharris.wixsite.com/selfknowledge) where she encourages her readers to dig into their roots. She can be followed on Twitter (@TiffanyAuthor88) and Instagram (@Tiffany_Author88). Interested readers can like her on Facebook, and subscribe to her YouTube channel (https://www.youtube.com/channel/UCYOM_4tVg465QQ39aJymiQA)

Printed in the United States
By Bookmasters